Gleanings of a Shepherd's Wife

Ibby MacIver

I humbly acknowledge my gratitude to Wemyss Billows for her initial invitation to speak at her meeting and her ongoing encouragement, which has been the springboard for all that has followed. I also acknowledge with heartfelt thanks the encouragement and gentle expert advice and help received from Sandra Bain in transferring my PowerPoint presentation to paper and her careful editing. I further acknowledge with deep gratitude the invaluable help received in several ways from nephew Roddy and his wife Fiona.

Photographs on page 36 and the back cover are © Roddy Mackay of Roddy Mackay Photography. Thank you, Roddy.
All other photographs are © Ibby MacIver

Scripture quotations marked NLT are taken from the Holy Bible, New Living Translation, copyright © 1996, 2004, 2015 by Tyndale House Foundation. Used by permission of Tyndale House Publishers, Inc., Carol Stream, Illinois 60188. All rights reserved

 "Scripture quotations marked ESV are from the ESV® Bible (The Holy Bible, English Standard Version®), copyright © 2001 by Crossway, a publishing ministry of Good News Publishers. Used by permission. All rights reserved."

Scripture quotations marked NIV are from THE HOLY BIBLE, NEW INTERNATIONAL VERSION®, NIV® Copyright © 1973, 1978, 1984, 2011 by Biblica, Inc.® Used by permission. All rights reserved worldwide.

ISBN 978-1-3999-2172-5

Published by Ibby MacIver. e: ibby.maciver@mailsaq.net t: 01463 731369

I dedicate this little book to my husband Donald

without whose hard work

none of this would have been possible

"Oh, I'm not!" This, with a vigorous shake of the head, was my immediate response to a friend in our Bible Study group when she suddenly asked me when I was coming to speak at her Women's Meeting.

She was very persistent so, with encouragement from others in the group, I agreed to go home and pray about it. It was coming up to lambing time and as I prayed about that request the Lord encouraged me and gave me this title: "*Gleanings of a Shepherd's Wife.*"

Gleanings are what I gathered over the following months as I watched, listened, questioned, but had minimal hands-on work with the sheep. I must make a disclaimer: I am *not* a shepherdess. But I am married to Donald, who has been farming full-time for the last 27 years here at '*Ashley*' farm on the Black Isle.

Donald's late sister, Isabel, had been the shepherdess but when she died in 1999, Donald inherited the care of the sheep to add to his work with cattle. Along with the sheep, Donald also inherited a very useful textbook – *The Veterinary Book for Sheep Farmers*.

Each year, during April lambing time, this book gets its annual airing. Even as I write, it is in use. I think the photo shows it has had a lot of use over several years!

But another textbook we both use daily is the Bible, where we are told:

"Acknowledge that the Lord is God. He made us and we are his. We are his people, the sheep of his pasture." Psalm 100 v 3 (NLT)

Over the ensuing months the Lord allowed me to have different, truly relevant experiences which enabled me to see even more clearly the parallels that exist between the work of the shepherd, the lives of the sheep, and what is recorded in the Bible. I'd like to share some of these lessons with you.

Without doing him an injustice, I know that Donald would not call himself a *good* shepherd, or a *great* shepherd – even after so many years, he's learning all the time. When something's gone wrong, and I've asked "Why?", he has often replied: "Poor shepherding!"
But the Bible does tell me of the

". . . Lord Jesus, (who is) the Great Shepherd of the sheep." Hebrews 13 v 20 (NLT) He says: "I am the Good Shepherd. I know my own sheep and they know me." John 10 v 14 (NLT)

Donald certainly does know his sheep though. Looking at some photos I had taken of the sheep, he could tell me: this one had twins; this one lost her lamb last year, and so on. They might all look alike to me, but to the shepherd they are all distinct individuals.

The Bible also says: *"He will feed his flock like a shepherd."* Isaiah 40 v 11 (NLT)

Donald's handbook tells him that sheep should be *called* to their food, not driven – and that's what Donald does. The bag is filled, the feeding troughs are cleaned, and he calls "Meh! Meh!", inviting the sheep to come. Food is about to be served and the sheep come to him.

I know this to be true, as I have tried calling to the sheep, attempting to emulate Donald's call of "Meh! Meh!" Some of the sheep ran from me, while others just ignored me! In order to take some of these photos, I had to dress in similar colours to Donald and go and sit in the field and just keep quiet.

The sheep recognise Donald's voice because they are familiar with it, and of course they associate that call with food. We too recognise the voices of those we know well and are familiar with. This makes me consider – am *I* close enough to my Good Shepherd to recognise his voice when he calls me? He also wants to supply my needs and feed me – with spiritual food.

"He calls his own sheep by name and leads them out." John 10 v 3 (NLT).

"Gannet" is the only name I can remember from Donald's flock, so named because she always was a greedy feeder. I find it wonderful, though, to realise that Jesus, the Good Shepherd, knows my name! I think sometimes he has to call my name at least twice, in order to get my attention.

"After he has gathered his flock, he walks ahead of them, and they follow him because they know his voice." John 10 v 4 (NLT)

The shepherd sometimes goes before his sheep and those who recognise his voice follow. They don't run ahead of him. They trust him to lead and guide them in the right way.

"He guides me along the right paths for his name's sake." Psalm 23 v 3b (NIV)

But some do stray! Sometimes, you'll get a sheep that doesn't listen to the shepherd and just likes to do its own thing. This can be a common enough sight on the roads of the beautiful west Sutherland, where a friend and I had gone for a day trip. This photo was taken through the car windscreen.

The next day, as I was continuing work on my presentation, God again gave me an experience so relevant to the task in hand.

"Some do stray"

It was one of those beautiful, warm days in June when all the windows and doors could be open. Donald was in a nearby field cutting grass for silage. Meg, the dog, was with him. I had gone to take them a drink. Coming home to continue my work, I headed for the computer in the den. As I passed the front door, I opened it wide and, as I climbed the stairs, said audibly to myself, "I hope we don't have any intruders."

I was working away happily when, suddenly, there was a crashing and banging downstairs! "What's wrong with Donald?" I exclaimed, jumping up to look out of the window to the field where he'd been working. He was still there, busy on the tractor. So, who was in the house? We had no children, and Donald had the dog with him. With my wee heart beating fast, I tiptoed quietly and slowly down the stairs. As I got to the foot of the stairs, I sensed that the noise was coming from the bathroom, which was almost directly opposite the open front door.

Nervously, I peeped round the door and what did I see but a sheep and two lambs! The lambs were grown lambs too. Not like these two by the side of the road in Sutherland. In my efforts to get them out of the house – with a trip through the living room and round the kitchen first – I quite forgot to find my camera!

I came across the following poem in a book just at that time too.

A Sheep...Not a Lamb!

'Twas a sheep, not a lamb, that went astray
In the parable Jesus told;
'Twas a grown-up sheep that wandered away
From the ninety and nine in the fold;

And out on the hilltop, and out in the cold,
'Twas a sheep that the good shepherd sought;
And back to the flock and back to the fold
'Twas a sheep that the good shepherd brought.

Now why should the sheep be so carefully fed
And cared for even today?
Because there is danger if they go wrong
They will lead the lambs astray.

The lambs will follow the sheep you know
Wherever they wander, wherever they go.
If the sheep go wrong, it will not be long
'Til the lambs are as wrong as they.

So still with the sheep must we earnestly plead
For the sake of the lambs today;
If the lambs are lost what a terrible cost
The sheep will have to pay.

Author Unknown

What a responsibility we all, as more mature "sheep", have in our dealings with youngsters, in whatever capacity that might be. If we go wrong, it won't be long before we lead the lambs astray, because

"All of us, like sheep, have strayed away. We have left God's paths to follow our own. . ." Isaiah 53:6 (NLT).

I am so grateful for the mature people who, over the years, have prayed for me and encouraged me back into the right way when I have gone, or been tempted to go, astray.

During the months of preparation, a friend and I visited a favourite old haunt of mine, in my homeland of Caithness. This is Holborn Head above Scrabster. We had gone prepared with binoculars and camera, expecting to see birds; I had not expected to see sheep on this dangerous headland, but God is a God of surprises and I have realised that his sheep and lambs are to be found scattered in unexpected places.

A straying lamb is here being watched by the mother.

This young one needs help, the mother decides, and she makes a move to come down to her lamb. She calls to the lamb, then turns and leads it away from the danger.

And look at the danger – one wee step more and this lamb would have been lost 200 feet down in the cold, often stormy, waters of the Pentland Firth.

The mother eventually leads the lamb down and across a hollow to join the others who are heading for new grazing. And it struck me that when we don't keep close to other members of the flock we can so easily be tempted to go astray. Temptations and dangers are just a step away.

We can see the sheep and the lambs here, but the shepherd is nowhere to be seen; and neither can we see the Good Shepherd today with our physical eyes. We walk by faith, not sight. In order to know what way to go we need to follow the example of the sheep.

". . . the sheep listen to his voice . . ." John 10 v3 (NIV)

So, we too have to learn to listen carefully, so that we recognise his voice as he leads and directs us through his word. Spending time sitting down with the Good Shepherd in prayer and Bible reading is vital for daily living as his sheep – and it is never time wasted.

Over the years I have not, for various reasons, had much direct hands-on involvement with the lambing, but I went out one morning to see what was happening in the 'Labour Ward'.

There were Donald and his nephew, with a ewe in labour. John was trying to save the lamb that was being presented head only, no front legs out, so it was stuck at the shoulders. After a struggle, he managed to pull the lamb free, but sadly its head had swollen too much and it died.

The men knew the ewe was going to have another lamb and decided to leave her to get on with that birth herself. John went away to his own work; Donald went to feed the ewes in the field, while I went to give water to those that had already lambed and were in their shed. Having finished my task, I returned to the 'Labour Ward' to check on the ewe, only to find that the second lamb had been born.

The 'Labour Ward'

However, it was still encased in the birth sac. Now, as I said, I am no shepherdess, but I knew enough to realise that I had to remove the birth sac from around the wee lamb's face and try to help it to breathe.

With no sign of life as I did that, I started to slap it – as I had watched the men do – to try to kickstart its heart. No response! I then lifted it up by the hind legs and swung it, head down, a few times; again as I'd seen the experts do. Still no sign of life in this little one! I had, sadly, failed to help this lamb live. I ran to tell Donald.

"Right. Adoption," he said. He went into the shed and picked up a pathetic wee lamb who wasn't thriving as its mother wasn't very well. Back to the 'Labour Ward' we went, and Donald proceeded to wash this sorry little lamb all over with the fluid from the birth sac of the dead lamb. It was then presented to the ewe who sniffed it – I wish I could imitate for you the sound that came from the ewe. In effect, what she was saying was, "Hello, little one! You are mine!" And we had a successful adoption.

That experience of a successful adoption spoke forcibly to me of my own adoption, not as a human child, but my adoption into God's family. My Bible tells me:

"God decided in advance to adopt us (me) into his own family by bringing us (me) to himself through Jesus Christ. . ." Ephesians 1:5 (NLT)

"Come now, let's settle this," says the Lord. "Though your sins are like scarlet, I will make them as white as snow. Though they are red like crimson, I will make them as white as wool." Isaiah 1 v 18 (NLT)

That adopted lamb was washed all over and thoroughly cleansed with the fluid from the birth sac of the dead lamb. So, too, does the blood of Jesus, the Lamb of God, who gave his life for me, cover over the stench of my sin. I could then be presented to and accepted by a Holy God as one of his children. Amazing!

In a similar picture, I also remember Isabel, my late sister-in-law, when she was the shepherdess, skinning a dead lamb. In a nearby pen there were triplets and the mother didn't have enough milk for all three. So, Isabel took one of them and put the coat of the dead lamb on it. She then presented that lamb to the ewe who had lost her own. The ewe sniffed the outer coat and, thinking it smelled like her lamb, she accepted it as her own.

When I am adopted into God's family, having confessed my sins, turned from them and been forgiven, I am covered with a new coat – the pure white wool of Jesus' righteousness. God doesn't see my sin, but instead sees the perfection of Jesus, his son.

"I am overwhelmed with joy in the LORD my God! For he has dressed me with the clothing of salvation and draped me in a robe of righteousness." Isaiah 61 v 10 (NLT). **What a gift!**

A favourite verse of mine is:

". . . this is what the Lord says 'Fear not, for I have redeemed you; I have called you by name; you are mine." Isaiah 43 v 1 (NIV).

I became a child of God and knowing God as my Father in heaven is a very precious thing to me. Adoption is a beautiful image for us to consider. I remember hearing of a teacher who, with her Primary 1 class, was looking at a family group photograph. "That girl's got different coloured hair," said Jamie. "Maybe she was adopted." "What does adopted mean?" asked Arnold. "I know," replied Mary. "I was adopted." The teacher asked her to tell the class what it meant to be adopted. "It means," said Mary, "that I grew in my Mummy's heart and not in her tummy."

Sometimes it's not too difficult to find lambs that have strayed a bit from the rest of the flock, and it was a relief to me when I found these two little ones!

I remember one year, when Donald was called away during lambing because his uncle had died. He had already been out earlier in the morning to check on the flock but was concerned to find that one ewe, who had had twins the night before, seemed to be missing one of them. So, I was despatched to go and look for the missing lamb. There was snow on the ground, and I walked all round the field anxiously looking for that lost lamb. Eventually, right at the top of the field, I found the sheep with her one lamb but not far away was a trail of blood in the snow — the fox had come visiting. I felt so sad over one lost lamb!

But when a lost lamb is found, "You are mine," is exactly what the shepherd says when he finds it. He's not content with the fact that the ewe still had the other twin, or that there are already lots of other lambs in the flock. No! He has to search for the lost one. His searching and seeking is not casual, but careful and thorough, with real longing in his heart to find the lost one.

"And when he has found it, he will joyfully carry it home on his shoulders. When he arrives, he will call together his friends and neighbours, saying, 'Rejoice with me because I have found my lost sheep.'" Luke 15 v 5,6 (NLT).

The Bible tells me that there is great rejoicing in Heaven over one sinner repenting – even more rejoicing over that one than over the 99 others, who had not strayed or got lost.

Working in the garden one morning, I became aware of more noise than usual – not just traffic on the busy road that runs through the farm, but also the bleating of lambs. I looked up to see black faces looking at me and calling from the other side of the fence. By the time I went to get my camera, they had turned the other way, but what they were calling was: *"Maa, Maa where's ma Maa?"*
The previous evening, Donald had separated the lambs from the ewes as they had to be weaned. Their mums were now well out of earshot.

"Maa, maa, where's ma maa?"

That made me think of what the Bible says about separation from God:

"It's your sins that have cut you off from God. Because of your sins, he has turned away and will not listen anymore."
Isaiah 59 v 2 (NLT)

Our sins separate us from God because, being holy, he cannot look on sin.

"But if we confess our sins to him, he is faithful and just to forgive us our sins and to cleanse us from all wickedness. 1 John 1: 9 (NLT)

When we have confessed our sins, turned from them, received forgiveness and know Jesus, the Good Shepherd to be our Saviour, then –

". . . nothing in all creation will ever be able to separate us from the love of God that is revealed in Christ Jesus our Lord." Romans 8 v 39 (NLT)

Nothing in life – or even death.

Besides lambing, another significant event in the shepherd's calendar is the sheep shearing. With warmer weather, the sheep have to be relieved of their thick woollen fleeces. Thankfully, Donald now calls in the help of a professional sheep shearer for what we call '*The Clipping*'. That's a great help! What would normally have taken him a few days on his own is now all over in less than a day.

'*The Clipping*'

On this day, I was there merely as a spectator, food provider and photographer. The flock had been gathered and there was a real noise of the bleating sheep. But as I watched and saw the way the sheep were handled – quite roughly really, I thought – and as I listened to the reaction of the sheep being clipped, I was conscious of the absence of any bleating from that particular animal. The sheep never opened its mouth. It was willingly accepting what the shearer was doing to it.

That spoke to me of Jesus.

"He was oppressed and treated harshly, yet he never said a word. He was led like a lamb to the slaughter. And as a sheep is silent before the shearers, he did not open his mouth." Isaiah 53 v 7 (NLT)

And as he, the sinless innocent Lamb of God, stood on trial before Pilate:

"So again, Pilate asked him, 'Aren't you going to answer? See how many things they are accusing you of.' But Jesus still made no reply, and Pilate was amazed." Mark 15 v 4,5 (NIV)

Jesus, though no fault could be found in him, made no attempt to defend himself against any of the accusations made because he knew he had come to suffer and die – for my sins and yours.

Another day, we were sitting at breakfast when there was the sound of bleating from a sheep in the field beyond the garden. "I'd know that voice anywhere," said Donald. "It's that small brown Suffolk. She always was a talkie sheep!"

He does know his sheep, I thought, not just when he sees them but when he hears them. I realised, that's the same with my Good Shepherd. Amazingly, Jesus hears my voice. He recognises my individual voice when I pray to him because, today, Jesus is alive and all my prayers and cries for help are passed through him to God in a way that God will accept. He's waiting and longing to hear from me – and to answer.

"In the morning, O Lord you hear my voice; in the morning I lay my request before you and I wait in expectation." Psalm 5 v 3 (NLT)

The shepherd will have been hearing the call of the sheep as they wait for their food. He will have taken note of their cry and be preparing to attend to it.

And expectation is rewarded! The answer does come. A good shepherd never fails to feed his sheep or respond to their call.

We, too, can pray or call to God with confidence, at any time. We know God hears and will answer in his time and way – the time and way he knows is right and best for his sheep – even if we have to wait a while for answers. But when the answers do come, then we will be able to say:

"God has surely listened and heard my voice in prayer." Psalm 66 v 19 (NIV)

A sheep or a lamb is not like a dog. You can't command a sheep to lie down. It will lie down of its own accord, when the right conditions have been provided by the shepherd; when it is well fed and content, it will chew the cud, chewing over and getting all the nourishment it can from the food it has received. When I saw this lamb lying in clover, chewing the cud, I found myself wondering if I also take time to carefully digest all that the Good Shepherd feeds me?

"He makes me lie down in green pastures" **is what the Bible says in** *Psalm 23 v 2a* **(NIV).**

How thankful I always am to have a warm and comfortable bed to lie down in each night!

But, also, we may have to lie down when the conditions are what we consider less than perfect. There are times when a shepherd has to take the sheep and make it lie down by turning it on to its back to deal with some problem it has; perhaps a sore foot. But when he does that, notice, the shepherd is still so close to the sheep. His hands are still on the sheep and the sheep's head is resting on the shepherd's knee.

When I read the words "He makes me lie down", or I see the sheep lying down, it reminds me of a time in my life when, for just over two years, about all I could do was lie down. But I well remember one morning, as I lay on the sofa not knowing what was wrong with me, I spoke to the Lord and said, "Lord, I don't know what's wrong with me. I don't know why I have to lie here. The medics don't know either. But I know that *you* know!" I just asked him to be with me – and he was.

The Great Shepherd provided the right conditions for me at that time. His hands were still on me. It was he who had made me lie down. He had work to do in me. He was the sovereign Lord and was still caring for me; he knew what I needed during that time.

I'm thankful to say that, during these months, I was enabled to know something of what Amy Carmichael spoke of when she wrote in her book, "Rose from Brier": "*Though through these months, acceptance has become a word of liberty, victory, and peace to me, it has never meant acquiescence in illness . . . But it did mean contentment with the unexplained.*"

Some versions of Scripture express the following verse differently:

"He refreshes my soul." Ps.23v3 (NIV). "He renews my strength" Ps. 23v3 (NLT). The Good Shepherd did both for me: he refreshed my soul, and he renewed my strength.

As I looked out of the window one evening, what caught my eye was not the sheep or the as-yet unploughed field, but the shadows. All of us have experienced shadows in our lives at one time or another. Times when we needed some extra special care and feeding.

Times when we needed to be carried; to know the support of strong loving arms around and underneath us. This reminds me of one of my favourite verses in Scripture: . . .

"He will carry the lambs in his arms, holding them close to his heart. . ." Isaiah 40:11 (NLT) **Who better to hug us or carry us?**

For some days, Donald had spent time giving special attention to a lamb that was struggling for life. Arriving home from church one Sunday morning, he ran in quickly to change his clothes and then went off outside. Some time later, wondering where he'd gone, this is what I saw when I went out to look for him. He was oblivious to my presence or the camera as I took this shot!

Even when a sheep or lamb may be dying, as this lamb was, and the shepherd has done all he can for the sheep, still he cares and is close by.

God has said,

'Never will I leave you; never will I forsake you.'"
Hebrews 13 v 5 (NLT).

The Good Shepherd really does care for his sheep.

Yes, sometimes these shadows can be really deep. I'm reminded of the psalm that is often referred to as the Shepherd's Psalm – Psalm 23 – where it says:

"Though I walk through the valley of the shadow of death, I will fear no evil; for you are with me . . ." (KJV)

We may question, "Why are there shadows in this field? What is causing there to be shadows here?" There is light from the sun. And if we know the Good Shepherd Jesus to be our Saviour, he will even be there with us in that valley as he promises, because *there can be no shadow without a light!* Jesus is there too. He has been there before us and is there to lead us through. Notepaper I received recently had this quote: "Turn your face to the sun and the shadows will fall behind you." The same is true if we turn our face to the Son of God, Jesus.

"There can be no shadow without a light."

We've learned a few lessons from looking at the sheep, but there are some lessons to be learned from the sheepdog too. No shepherd is complete without a sheepdog, although I did hear of a young girl who thought that Jesus could not possibly be a Good Shepherd! Why? Because he didn't have a dog! But she was told, perhaps wisely, "Oh he had two! They were called 'Goodness' and 'Mercy'!" The 23rd Psalm finishes with these words:

"Surely goodness and mercy shall follow me all the days of my life." Psalm 23 v 6 (KJV)

This is Meg, as a young pup, asleep in her feeding bowl. Before I took this photo, she was asleep on top of a ewe that was in the pen with her, so either she was on top of the job or asleep on the job!

Now, some years later, here is Meg keeping her eye on the sheep as they keep their eyes on her, holding them there so that the shepherd can come and pick out the one needing some special attention. She's also keeping an eye on her master, ready to obey. Meg is Donald's right-hand companion, happiest when obeying her master's commands – those commands that she has been taught from a young age.

My Good Shepherd is looking for the same delighted obedience from me to His commands too.

"Those who accept my commandments and obey them are the ones who love me." John 14 v 21 (NLT) "I take joy in doing your will, my God, for your instructions are written on my heart." Psalm 40 v 8 (NLT)

Is that true of me, I wonder?

The shepherd doesn't always take his dog with him, as it depends on where he is going. On such days, Meg, weather permitting, lies at the foot of our road watching and waiting for her master's return. When I saw her there one day, and took this photo, the words that came to me were "What a faithful friend!" and then this line of a hymn popped into my mind: "Faithful One, so unchanging..." And that Faithful One is of course . . .

. . . "Jesus Christ [who] is the same yesterday, today, and for ever." Hebrews 13 v 8 (NLT)

What better friend could I have: so unchanging, always the same, always there.

Looking at Meg as she lay there, I was also struck by her pose. She was very alert. She was watching – eyes open, listening with her ears up – patiently waiting, not restless or fretting, not asleep. And her paws were ready for action – confidently expecting and waiting for the return of the shepherd, her master whom she would gladly welcome back. Is my attitude the same with regards to the return of my Good Shepherd, Jesus?

"For the Son of Man will come with his angels in the glory of his Father and will judge all people according to their deeds." Matthew 16 v 7 (NLT)

"You also must be ready all the time, for the Son of Man will come when least expected." Matthew 25 v 44 (NLT)

I've used this picture elsewhere in this book, but as I'm looking at it again, I'm noticing that, amongst this wee flock of sheep, there are different colours of faces.

There are the white faces of the North Country Cheviots and the black faces of the Suffolks. These are only two breeds out of over 1000 distinct breeds that are estimated to exist worldwide, displaying a huge variety of shape, size and colour.

I can also see that there is a difference in the ages of the animals in this flock: there are the mature ewes and even a young lamb. What may not be so obvious is that there are male and female animals too. The large black face at the back is the male Suffolk ram or tup; the others are the female ewes. So, there is quite a mixture in this small flock!

It's not easy to count the number of sheep in this flock but we could perhaps come up with an approximate guesstimate – around 24? But in looking at this little flock that Donald was working with, it made me think of what the Bible says about the complete flock that the Good Shepherd will have gathered in when God's Kingdom comes?

"After this I saw a great crowd, too many to count, from every nation and tribe and people and language, standing in front of the throne and before the Lamb." Revelation 7: 9 (NLT)

In that gathering, there will be people of all colours, shapes and sizes, all tribes and nations and ages, male and female. And there will be far too many to count! But we can't see that great crowd yet. That's something to look forward to.

If you were to ask Donald, "Is this your whole flock?", he would say, "No! I have sheep grazing in other fields too." Over the summer months he rents grazing pasture from neighbouring farmers. To bring his whole flock together, these sheep would also have to be rounded up and gathered in. And what does Jesus the Good Shepherd say about His flock just now?

"I have other sheep, too, that are not in this sheepfold. I must bring them also. They will listen to my voice, and there will be one flock with one shepherd." John 10 v 16 (NLT)

Although Donald's flock is relatively small, he still needs help to gather them in. Thankfully he has his trusted helper, Meg, the sheepdog. Although Meg is not to be seen in this photo, that doesn't mean she's not at work. The flock have come together, are moving as one and the shepherd looks fairly relaxed.

Yes, Meg is there and doing what she can to help as a loyal, faithful, active friend and supporter. She's using her God-given instincts and remembering what she's been taught.

Although she wasn't to be seen in the last picture, the shepherd can still see her. And she's in a position where she can hear her master's instructions – her ears are attuned to his voice and she is ready to obey and do what she can to help the shepherd, her master, gather in the flock.

Am I in a similar position in relation to my Good Shepherd is what I'm asking myself? Are you? Like Meg, your help may not be given in an up-front, high-profile position to be seen by others, but the Good Shepherd will see and will have taken note of it. Perhaps you are working away prayerfully in the background, but in so doing fulfilling an indispensable role. What you can do may seem insignificant to you, but not to Jesus.

On one occasion, when I shared the presentation, I had taken a friend with me who said to me afterwards, "I could never do that!" This friend had been a District Nurse and a Marie Curie Nurse. My thoughts were, I could never have done *that!* But we need to remember Meg! She couldn't drive the tractor, open the gates or feed the sheep, but she used the gifts, the instincts and training she did have.

"She has done what she could. . ." Mark 14: 8a (NLT)

I'd probably read these words many times before, but I was made particularly aware of them not long after that conversation with my friend. It was that occasion in Bethany, in the home of Simon the leper. While Jesus was reclining at the table, a woman, Mary, came and anointed Jesus' head with very costly ointment. That may have been a gift to her, but she was happy to use it for her Lord. When others scolded her for "wasting" it, as they thought, Jesus rebuked them and, commending her, said, "She has done what she could."

The challenge for me is, have I? Have I done all I could to help bring lost and straying "lambs" into the safety of the fold of God's love?

These then are some of my gleanings as a shepherd's wife! As with any gleanings, I have gathered up some, but I trust that I've left some for you to take away, which will be a blessing to you.

I am thankful to have been able to share with you as someone who can unashamedly and very gratefully say, "The Lord is my Shepherd."

"The Lord is my Shepherd"